In Which I Try to Save the World

Part-Time Poets

Collection I

Copyright © 2024 Part-Time Poets Press

ISBN: 9798301164101

All rights reserved

Book cover designed in Canva by Michelle Windsor

Book title from the poem by Krista Dreschel (page 27)

First paperback edition December 2024

Dedicated to our notes apps

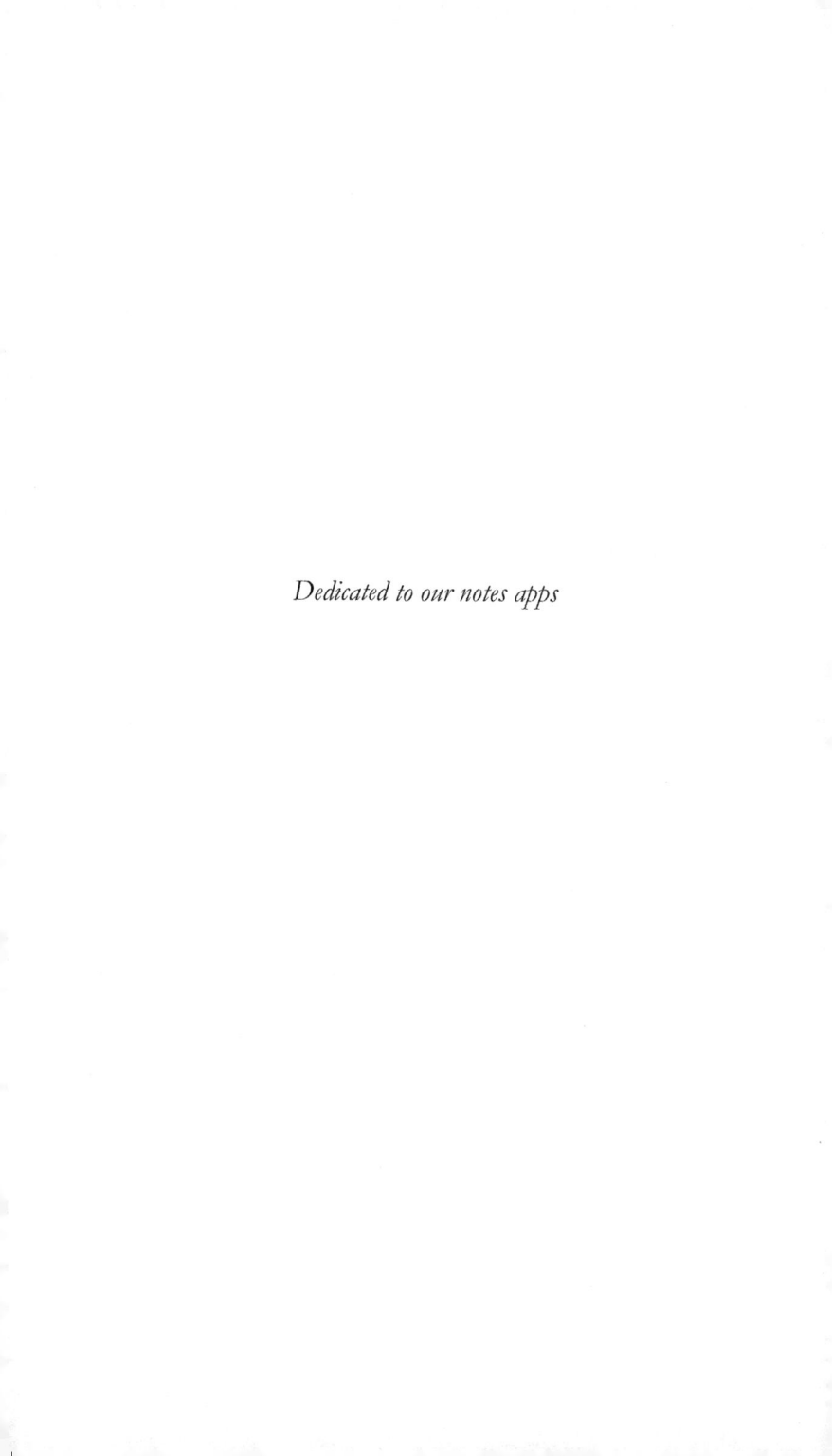

INTRODUCTION

"The genesis of a poem for me is usually a cluster of words. The only good metaphor I can think of is a scientific one: dipping a thread into a supersaturated solution to induce crystal formation. I don't think I solve problems in my poetry; I think I uncover the problems."
Margaret Atwood

In the spring of 2019, I was an exhausted mother of two working full time and struggling to write creative nonfiction essays. I wanted to write, I needed to write, and yet every time I tried my sentences came out half-formed and my word count too short.

That's when I discovered I could write poetry.

Poetry doesn't demand complete sentences, punctuation, 1500 words, or an introduction and conclusion. It simply asks: *What do you see? What do you feel? What do you want?*

The poems in this collection were written between April 2023 and December 2024 by nine writers who are also women and mothers, women who, in the margins of their sacred, full, and messy days, dared to answer poetry's questions.

I hope you can find a few poems here that make you say, "Yes, me too," and if you do, I encourage you to hold on to them. Take them with you into your own sacred, full, and messy days.

Sending you strength and peace,

Michelle Windsor
Creator of Part-Time Poets

Contents

Mothering	**1**
They Say Motherhood Kills Your Creativity	3
Oxygen	4
Synaptic Pruning	5
I Daydream About Running Away	6
My Husband Resents the Children	8
Evidence	9
If a Mother Walked on the Moon	10
Fire Safety	12
(s)mother	13
The Gulf's Gift	14
Baby Teeth	15
Raging	**17**
Red Ink	19
The Art of the Kill	20
Nice Girls Don't Get Angry	21
The Smallest Man Who Ever Lived	22
Grieving	**23**
When My Children Ask About Death	25
In Which I Try to Save the World	27
Please, Don't Ask	29
Red Notebook	31
Let Me Tell You How It Ends	32
Hoping	**33**
Fake It 'Til You Make It	35
Just Like Light	36

Little Pockets of Happiness	37
The Dance	38
Bloom	39
Hope	41
Being	**43**
Cheap Thrills	45
I Don't Go To Visit Guilt; She Lives Here	46
Proof of Life	48
Dear Influencer	49
Osmosis or Middle Age	50
After Watching the Little Mermaid, My Daughter Asks About Her Voice	51
Listen to Your Body	52
A Married Thursday, Nine Years In	53
In A World Where You Can Be Anything, Be Weak	54
Planning on Wrinkles	55
About The Authors	**57**

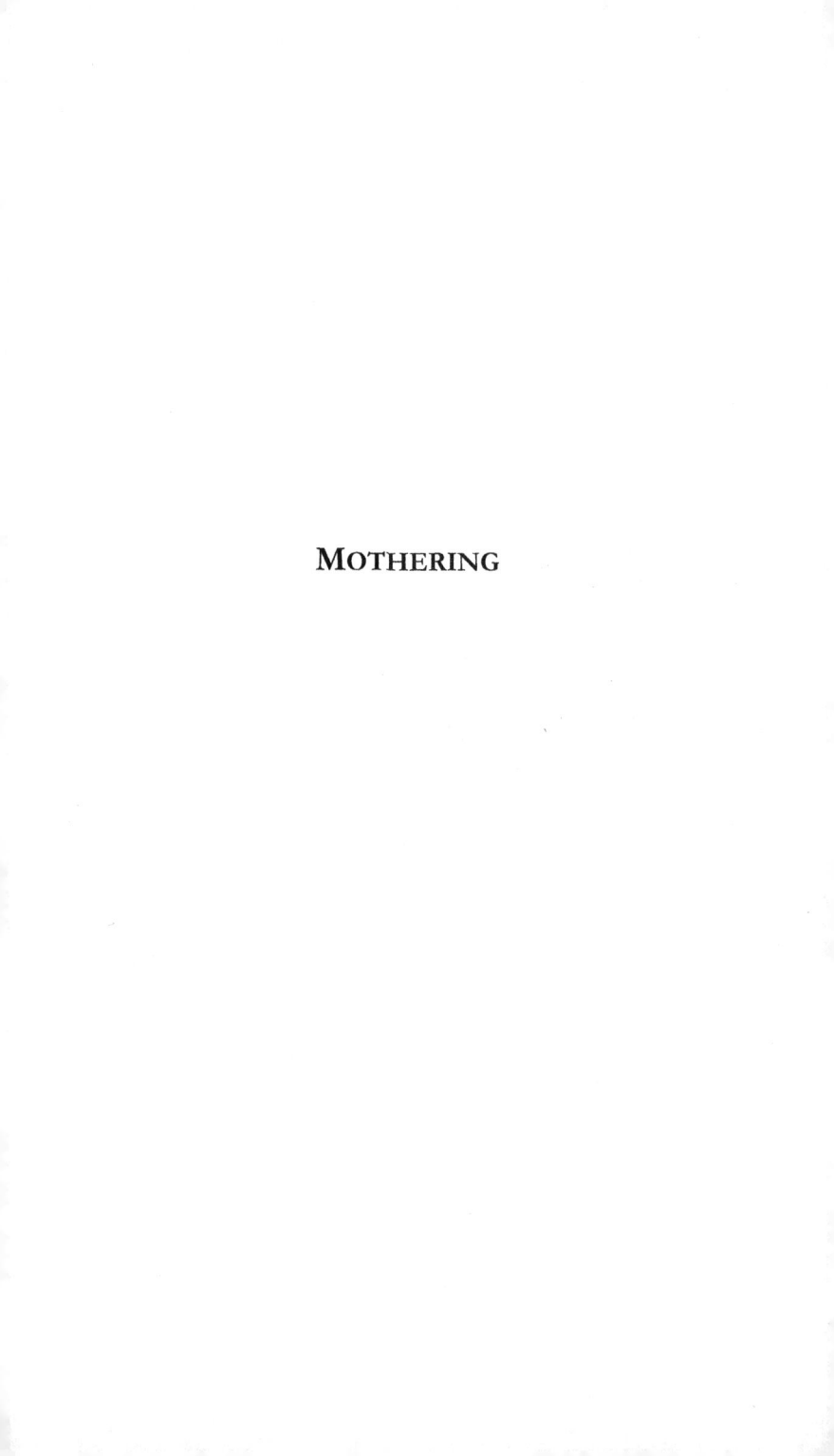

MOTHERING

They Say Motherhood Kills Your Creativity

But just the other day, I samba'd while rocking my daughter
to sleep. Wrote poems in the dirt with my son.

Drew pictures of a giraffe on a lunch note napkin.
Last week, I put on a live performance

in the living room—called it Musical Mom.
It's not the best thing I've ever written, but it's certainly

not the worst. I have spent hours fingerpainting and sidewalk-
chalking, dancing under the disco lights in Barbie's dream house,

crooning in the kitchen while making scrambled eggs. Mothers,
gather round—I am telling you some truths:

Creativity doesn't sink in the mud of motherhood,
doesn't scuff up your Sunday shoes. It simply shifts, a subtle

trick of the light, a snake shedding its skin.
An artist painting the great work of her life.

Jillian Stacia

Oxygen

No matter how many kids fill your house,
they'll fill your hours. Like air—
a gas will expand to fill a container.
A body will mine its own bones
to feed a growing child. A mother
will strip away everything she thought
she needed to live   and still
live, propelled by purpose. A little god
to serve with wholehearted devotion.
Brittle bones and lank hair, offerings
on the altar, sanctified and sanctifying.
Necessary as the air in her lungs.

Lorren Lemmons

Synaptic Pruning

The brain prunes past pains
and I'm happy to lose those,
but what if it prunes
the memory of your toes?
Those ten tiny toes
that wiggle and wave,
they're the memory
I'd most like to save.
I'm happy to lose
chemistry, countries,
and even my shoes.
But those toes, those toes,
and how tiny you are,
nestled here on my chest.
I know what it means
to be idle and blessed.

Rebecca Fergie

I Daydream About Running Away

I'll leave a note—love you,
don't miss me, I'll be back in 3 weeks,
6 weeks tops—and my phone.
I'll take my passport
and cash out of the ATM.
I'll abandon the minivan in the garage
and order an Uber.

Airport, please.
Where are you going?
I'm not sure yet. The next flight.

I'm tired

of squeezing each day like a wet towel
trying to extract every drop of productivity.

When the plane departs
I leave behind
        expectations
        efficiency
        grief (in all the big and small ways)
        smiles
small talk
        holding it all together.

When I arrive, I
dry my hair in the breeze
and embrace the open air.
Wear bright pink lipstick for myself
and jangle bangles up to my elbow.
Bear my midriff (I've still got it!)
with a long skirt that flirts with the waves.

I sit down to dinner
say "fuck you" to the calories.
I tear apart brioche with my teeth
and suck butter off shrimp caught from the sea.
I order double chocolate cake for dessert
and lick the plate clean.

The next morning
I sleep until the sun is high in the sky
order a full fat double shot latte
read a pile of books in bed.
I look in the mirror—
at my fresh wrinkles and wiry gray
hair along my part—
and grin.

Welcome home.

Alyssa Silvester

My Husband Resents the Children

for growing up. For their pudgy limbs
lengthening, growing stronger,
less wobbly. For their love twisting
into something complicated, cagey, harder
to satisfy. Snacks and rattles no longer
stop tantrums; anger doesn't dissipate
overnight—it thickens into a knot
under their hardening ribcages.

Still, I marvel
at their roughened skin, the wings
of shoulders once folded within
me. How they used to need my body,
but now they mostly need my phone.
How the sun freckles their noses.
How I cannot shield them. My influence wanes
like a sickling moon. Once my seedlings,
they've bloomed into strange, looming trees.
My arms long for the universe once contained
easily. Still, I wander under their shade,
rooted in their own soil, and stand in awe.

Lorren Lemmons

Evidence

Show me your living room on a Friday morning. The laundry napping on the couch. Legos building dreams. Show me your kitchen after you make your favorite meal. Bowls dripping and counters sticky. Dirty dishes waiting for you to come back from the feast. Show me the crumbs on the floor, the unmade beds, the shoes piled by the door, the toothpaste smeared on the sink. Show me the broken crayons and the art on the walls. Show me your desk covered with pieces of yourself waiting to be put into poems. Show me the transcripts of the arguments and the tapes of the belly laughs. Show me the evidence.

Michelle Windsor

If a Mother Walked on the Moon

"Swish whaaa CHA! Swish whaaa CHA!"

"What's that sound?"

"That's the sound of someone walking on the moon," she proclaimed confidently, bouncing from the backseat while we waited in the school dropoff line.

"Oh, that's interesting. I have no basis for knowing if that's actually true. I've never walked on the moon."

"Do you think you might? Ya know, walk on the moon?"

"I mean, I have lots of years in front of me. So, I'm not exactly ruling out the possibility."

"If my mother walked on the moon, I would sing, 'My mother is on the moon! What a surprise! What a surprise!'"

And what a surprise it would be to feel the way that moondust cuts, razor sharp to start, but a source and force and for so much fluidity.

I would feel compelled to tell her, "I'm a woman, too."

But she'd already know that by the gentle assertion of my step and my hostess gift of actual cheese. We'd bubble it over ancient lava, bring laughs to the gas, and wonder why it's taken so long for me to arrive, because if it's always been about balance ... a mother would certainly know best.

Then, while wiping molten gruyere from the corners of my mouth, I'd politely ask, "Could you give me a minute?" while gesturing in the general direction of the Earth.

"Why of course. Take your time."

And I would look out and talk to her, you know, mother to mother.

"While I have you, I just want to say I'm sorry about the fragmented forests and the wildfires and the tsunamis and the oil and the coal and …

"And the plastics? Tell me you're sorry about the plastics."

"I absolutely am sorry about the plastics. I recycle … and I use zero-waste natural deodorant and I'm thinking about a bamboo toothbrush, but I'm just one person. A mother at that, with mouths to feed and fights to break up and laundry to fold. And if I could multiply, divide and conquer … if I could lower the temperature and soften all the edges all alone … I would. But that would be such an unprecedented surprise … like Artemis going first, for the first and last time, because she had to help Apollo be born."

"Darling, puhhhlease don't get so emotional. The world is watching."

Swish whaaa CHA.
Swish whaaa CHA.

Megan Sciarrino

Fire Safety

These days our life is highly flammable
In the way that small children are always combustible

Their needs the flames that lick at my consciousness
Their troubles the smoke that clouds my sight
Exhaustion poured over all of it like gasoline
You and I two fire chiefs with hoses at the ready

At night we fall into bed bone-tired
Our scorched hands finding each other
And there among the ashes we whisper
"Don't you think the inferno is actually kind of beautiful?"

Tomorrow the alarm will sound
And we'll once again don our turnout gear
But tonight our dreams are populated
By the arresting charm of dancing flames

Amy Grass

(s)mother

I have this urge
to swallow you
up inside my skin—
this shaking
body suddenly
preferable
to the messy
madness
of the outside
world. Bone
of my bone, blood
of my blood: loving
you is muscle
memory. Mothers
make the best
houses. Let me
build you a city
inside my skeleton,
each vessel a brick,
each vein a victory
song shouting only
your name. I'd give
you the world,
but what is it offering?
Better to bet
on the body
that beats only
for you. Listen,
do you hear it? Every
cell says to stay.

Jillian Stacia

The Gulf's Gift

Emerald water stretches,
folds over herself
like dimpled baby thighs.
Runs like a child,
foams at our ankles,
laps our feet, trying to hold
on while she freefalls.
Our toes sink into playdough.

She retreats and reveals
a half-hidden white seashell.
My son bends and digs.
Droplets cling
to the bottom of his lobes.

He plucks the shell,
places it in my palm.
I turn it over. A perfect curve
mimics his ear. Its silky interior
like stroking his cheek.
The back ridges like his fingerprint.

"Come on, Mama, let's jump!"
The wind carries his voice,
and he races into crashing waves.
I clutch the seashell in one hand
and run after him into the water.

Alyssa Silvester

Baby Teeth

Each morning, I lift my son's
cracked molar from my jewelry tray,
rub my fingers against the pearled
enamel, thumb catching
over the ridges. I find teeth
everywhere, these days—
castoff shells as he ebbs
and flows through the house
like a tide. One on his desk, another
in a plastic bag on the kitchen counter.

You've heard of mothers-in-law gifting
their sons' brides with boxes or baggies
or necklaces of teeth, passing the torch
of loving his body, shaped so carefully
in the womb's oyster shell, the grit
of morning sickness and sciatica
rolled into a priceless pearl,
fashioned cell by cell.

My mother kept my umbilical stump
in a plastic case on her vanity—
a wizened raisin, leathery
with old blood. I tell the story
to laugh at the absurdity of mothers,
our stubborn clinging to the driftwood
of the past. But here I stand,
unable cast off his relics,
watching him grow tall and untethered.

Lorren Lemmons

Raging

Red Ink

I am full of love poems
and rage[1] and words

that never made it to the page
because I was afraid

of what you might think,
what you might say.

This is the curse
of being a writer,

of being a woman,
of being.

At night I carve sentences
into the headboard,

and in the the morning
sand them into dust.

Mix the dust with all the
red ink I have spilled

editing myself down
from a fucking epic poem

into a nursery rhyme
just so you would feel fine.

Michelle Windsor

---

[1] "I am full of love poems and rage" from @sunlightafterdark
https://www.instagram.com/p/C_04zL9ywU_/?img_index=1.

The Art of the Kill

The other day I learned that it's the mother
orca who teaches her baby girl how to hunt—

fin cutting through obsidian ocean,
open-jawed and opal-eyed, transcending this world

of shark and men, becoming the hunter
instead of the hunted, becoming something else

entirely. The other day I learned you can poke out an eye
with the jab of the thumb, break a nose with the heel

of your Sunday school palm, buy a little blade
to hook through your keys. I wonder

when I'll show you how to survive
this world of shark and men—how to smile

through sharp teeth, stay small
in a crooked current, snarl without making a sound.

Am I a better mother for teaching you the art of the kill?
Or is pointing out the poison its own kind of death—

the sort of pain you never unsee?
The orcas smile in my sleep.

They do not question the nature of things,
know every mother has just one wish for her daughter:

survival

Jillian Stacia

Nice Girls Don't Get Angry

Anger stabs me above my eye, but I don't
listen because nice girls don't get angry

Anger aches and shakes my jaw, but I don't
listen because nice girls don't get angry

Anger severs the connection between my brain
and my words. I can't talk, but I don't listen
because nice girls don't get angry.

Anger seeps into my neck, shoulders, tense,
tightening, curling, screaming. But I don't listen
because nice girls don't get angry.

Anger tries again, searing a highway
down my chest. But I don't listen,
because nice girls don't get angry.

Anger descends to my stomach, a roiling,
boiling, nauseous toiling, but I don't listen
because nice girls don't get angry.

I'm fine. I'm just ignoring my friend who tells
me this is not okay. I can't open the door,
so I bar it with my body, sob while she kicks

and screams, "Don't do this!" on the other side
because all I want is for you to think I'm nice.

Rebecca Fergie

The Smallest Man Who Ever Lived

was still a giant
among women.
boys will be *boys*
will be boys until
they grow up to
become crooked
men—CEO.
Supreme Court Justice.
President of the Free World.
tale as old as time.
let's skip
to the end:
no one believes
her. if this breaks
your heart, let it.
women are burned
at the stake every day
just for trying
to survive. I'm sick
of choking on
secondhand
smoke from inferior
men. go ahead,
set me on fire.
haven't you heard?
we're already
burning.

Jillian Stacia

GRIEVING

When My Children Ask About Death

A cloudless blue sky stretches overhead on a short walk
to the lake, and my daughter points to roadkill.
Her pigtails the color of sunshine overhead kiss

the tops of her shoulders with her movement. I can't stop
her. She charges toward the decaying brown fluff
and shouts, "That squirrel is dead!"

She talks about the dead squirrel for the next three months.

On Wednesday's drive to school, my son asks, "When am I going to die?"
My eyes widen, grip tightens on the steering wheel.
Before I can answer, he proclaims, "Dad will die first, he's the oldest."

My heart rips open, perforated paper torn from a notebook.
How can I explain tragedy to a kindergartner?
Maybe Dad won't die first.

I choke on the thought like a grape. I want to imagine other outcomes.

Tragedy is real.
Death is real.
Is life simply a highway to a graveyard?

Wind swirls and calls for leaves to waltz, colors swishing like gowns around ankles.
Sun saturates the sky in the exact color of watermelon juice dripping down my daughter's chin.
You encircle my shuddering shoulders, absorbing my body's earthquake of grief.
I blow raspberries on my son's soft belly until laughter explodes like champagne.
Pop!

You tap caramelized sugar on crème brulée. Crack! Sweet & bitter dissolves on your tongue.

I fall asleep on lavender-scented sheets, my husband's body curled around mine like a comma.

Morning sun slants through pines in my backyard until every tree is drenched with light.

I step barefoot into dew- soaked grass, watch squirrels jump like Olympians branch to branch.

Woodpeckers create morning metronomes, and I consider.

We will all die.
Even you.
Even me.

Can I look out the window to notice—lipsticked leaves, honey-colored sunlight, uncontainable laughter—in the midst of roadkill? Can the beauty of this moment soften my heart's ache?

Alyssa Silvester

In Which I Try to Save the World

At noon, the sky turns itself inside out,
rain pelting pumpkins on the stoop.
The children did not know the sun

could disappear so suddenly,
but I have seen this before.
"Come here. You are safe,"

I say over the downpour, scooping
my children into my lap. Somewhere
there are mothers who want to do this

but can't. Somewhere there are children
who want to feel this but won't.
All this talk about tending to our own

circles of influence, and all I want is to gather
the whole world into my arms like this,
sit on the cold kitchen tile, spine pressed

against stainless steel, lunch left
burning on the stove. My mother-in-law
tells me we already have a savior,

and I know she's right. I know God does not
need me, but still I try. Still, I erase the jagged
lines, press hard like my kindergartner—

paper ripping, hole widening, and still I keep going,
pink rubber against the page. The quesadillas
turn black on the stove, and I let them.

What is urgent, really?
That you stay alive.
And you. And you.

Krista Drechsel

Please, Don't Ask

In the early morning hours
their questions haunt me

"Don't you want more?"

It's not a matter of *wanting*.
In all my growing up
I wanted to be an author
and a mother

A mother with a house full
of children
running
and laughing
and playing
and all mine

My heart aches
for the children I
may never get to hold
as long as this sickness
continues to control my mind
I would rather be here and alive
with my one daughter
and playing
and creating
and laughing
and living
than gone
with more left behind.

Sometimes
I wonder if it would
be different than the first time

now that I have support
now that I am a mother
now that I know how to take
care of the anxiety
and depression
and suicidal ideation
and loneliness

But
I'm not ready
to cling to that
hope
not ready
to wish for
a different brain.

So instead, I plead
Please, don't ask.

Taylor Epperson

Red Notebook

I want to tell my children they have nothing to fear
but I still remember
the signal for an intruder
at my elementary school
Mrs. Crumby has lost her red notebook

I parse out tragic headlines
debating which information to relay
and which to withhold, preserving
some semblance of innocence for a little
while longer

At night I sit on the edge of the bathtub
while they brush their teeth,
catching the last dregs of the day's musings
and I let myself imagine
the world as the gentle place they hope for it to be

Amy Grass

Let Me Tell You How It Ends

it ends in loss, death, brown piles of decay
that leaf you crushed under your boot and watched

the wind carry away—gone—just like that belief
you crumpled up and let go last week

you want a happy ending, an easy button, a fast-
forward option, but you can't skip this part

you're stripped bare now
there's nothing left to hide behind

it's going to get colder and darker
so no, I'm not going to give you a fairy tale

that leaf is not coming back
but something new, something different is

waiting—so watch
for that first sign of green

for the unfurling
slowly, painfully at first

and then
and then

Michelle Windsor

HOPING

Fake It 'Til You Make It

One hundred times a day I am a hypocrite,
imploring my children to house more hope
in their little bodies than I have ever let in.
I whisper promises of happy endings
during scary scenes, though I myself curl
my insides into fists, bracing for the day
my words ring hollow in the space between
us. I point to a coneflower, a crow, a cloud
shaped like a turtle, as if I do not also go on
and on behind closed doors, spewing over
the specific hells one twenty-four-hour day
in America has wrought. Still, I tell my children
God is kind to them, so it is the last thing
they hear before they fall asleep, though
I myself tally on my fingers all the people
who stand poised and eager to tell them
otherwise, all the people who, even now,
are saying in so many slippery ways:
Well, now, it depends. Anyone will tell
you the first week at a new job to fake
it 'til you make it, and isn't that what I am
doing now? Faking it. Making it. Shielding
my tender hope until it can stand
on its own. Saying the words
until I believe them.

Krista Drechsel

Just Like Light

Once, a church organ made music within the chambers of my heart.

And I no longer wonder how things grow.

Because love, in all its forms, be it peonies, paint, piccolos, pause, or salt and pepper, spills

just
like
light.

Megan Sciarrino

Little Pockets of Happiness

Leaving the last few pages of a book until tomorrow so tomorrow will be good / when my daughter points me out to all of her friends as I drive up in the car line / the article about a woman from my church my husband sent me that makes me feel seen / the text that says "I miss you" / "how are you" / "want to go to lunch?" / the warmth of the morning sunrise on my face/ the crisp air outside when I get the mail / leaves changing their color / when the cat wants to snuggle / a good cry / a good therapy session / clarity / questions / wondering what other pockets of joy I'll find today

Taylor Epperson

The Dance

She spins—
shards of light
shatter
darkness
dissipates.

Sun rises
and sunflowers search.

Blaze beguiles
and heads swing.

Stalks stake nightwatch
until blooms wake

dripping
dropping
drooping—

      waiting

              to

                        drink

the light.

Alyssa Silvester

Bloom

The carnation buds have not yet begun
to open their puckered mouths.

They are pregnant with the promise
of blooming, but it is cold,
and they are not yet ready.

My daughter cups each one
in her tiny palm, whispers—
It's ok, you can grow.

She breathes gently
on the plant's tight little fists,
even though I have never
taught her to do this,
even though I kill every flower I touch.

The world has a bitter bite, now.
It chomps at my heels—
the reason I lace up my shoes
and run until I cannot breathe.

But here in my own kitchen
is a tender beholding,
a gentle exhale, an open palm
holding stubborn possibility.

Do you see?

There is still some kindness left.
There still remain those who will bend
to help another soul bloom.

This is what I think about
as I finally slow to a walk,
as I pass under the weeping willow,
as its branches bend to stroke my hair
like a mother.

Krista Drechsel

Hope

A tiny, fickle thing

Until it sticks to you

Like glitter.

An explosion

Of color and sparkle,

You can't get rid of it,

Even if you tried.

And why would you?

It's stunning.

Taylor Epperson

BEING

Cheap Thrills

I'm a cautious person
but once in a while I cut loose

and eat raw cookie dough
ignore a sign that says no right on red
return a library book a few days late
click "agree" without reading the terms and conditions.

I might drink coffee after noon
let the kids watch a show before 5 p.m.
go to bed without washing my face
buy a dress I don't need just because I like how it swishes around my legs

watch out world
I think I might tell someone how I really feel
laugh louder than necessary
ask for what I want
give without expectation of getting back

What was that?
Did you say something?
I couldn't hear you over the sound of my
living.

Amy Grass

I Don't Go To Visit Guilt; She Lives Here

I don't know how she got in, but she likes to call out the dust on my blinds, the dishes in my sink, the tone in my voice.

I tick something off the list. Guilt slips her arm over my shoulder, whispers in my ear about the three other things I didn't do.

When I get something done, she slips into bed next to me, touches my face, and says, "But honey, you didn't do it very well."

Guilt brings her friends over. Pride laughs, "You don't need help, you just need to work harder."

Guilt says, "Don't tell your friends. You're wasting their time. It's not bad enough."

Impatience drums her fingers on the dresser and sighs, "You should have it together by now."

Guilt says, "You've done it wrong,"

but Shame sneers, "You are wrong,"

I am heavy, my limbs are calling, crying to commune with the floor, the effort to remain vertical is becoming more and more.

I tell my husband about my guest. He says her name is Guilt. He says she doesn't stay with him.

It's like learning the sky isn't blue.

He says she has another name. He calls her the Accuser.

He reminds me of a better Name. The One who paid my debt. The One who doesn't scorn.

The One who says, "My grace is sufficient for you. My power is made perfect in weakness."

When Guilt comes to the door, I boast gladly of my flaws, then I go inside the house.

Christ says, "That's enough,"

and slams the door in her face.

Rebecca Fergie

Proof of Life

the gray hairs
sprout
like wildflowers across my
head.
a part of my mind whispers
but you aren't even 30 yet.
i push it away—
grateful for every
wry, shiny hair that glitters
in the sun.

Taylor Epperson

Dear Influencer

Goddess of algorithms, Hestia of the pixelated screen,
cast your golden net of perfection over me.
Illuminate your ways—the fingerprint-free refrigerator door,
the gleaming toilet bowl. Show me how you conjure
steaming nourishment for your families, plated
and served on a pristine hearth. Style
my family in bamboo cotton, filter my blemishes, smooth
my cellulite. Brew me the elixir
that makes your husband smile   like that.
Grant me a grid of perfection, color-matched and set
to music. Soundtrack my life, craft
me a narrative. Don't crack
the glass—just let me through
the portal, into the magic
of the world you're showing me.

Lorren Lemmons

Osmosis or Middle Age

I don't know if it's osmosis or middle age or a membrane somewhere in between,
but the ocean billows my body like linens on a clothesline.

It circles my ribs around my back and brings my breast forward and ushers a well in my throat.

I didn't have the years to know her this way when I was young
and giving
and giving
and giving
my brow to the sun.

Now I wear a hat and I ask the horizon,
Is this my homecoming?
Do I cry because I remember arriving?
Do I cry because the cradle is so gentle?
Do I cry because I try to make my heart a coffer for all the firsts and all the lasts?

And she replies with the fizzle of white crests,
telling my mind to
rest
rest
rest.

Megan Sciarrino

After Watching the Little Mermaid, My Daughter Asks About Her Voice

But where does it live?

She means, *Where in the body?*
She means, *Is it an organ like the heart?*
She means, *Can it be held hostage?*

I could tell her all the people
who may prefer her voice box to be a cage,
her throat to be a prison, all the people

who may steal her words and hold them
captive in their own slippery mouths.
I could tell her all the ways I still scrape

the words caught under my own tongue,
all the ways I still twist the rusty key
to let the truth go free. I could tell her

all the times I say to myself Good God
Almighty, she's going to need this,
all the times I will her to memorize

the exact shape of her voice, feel its heft,
ask others to hold it in their hands.
I could tell her all of this, but I still believe

in the power of a happy ending—good
defeating evil, the voiceless finally
heard, the singing loud and triumphant.

So I tell her, *Put your hand here. Can you feel,
can you see? This is your voice. It is yours to keep.*
And she sings and she sings and she sings.

Krista Drechsel

Listen to Your Body

when your knees start aching
the day before the weather changes
or when your stomach churns
after you've been fed bad theology

when your hips sway, nodding
in approval at the dress you just slipped
over them, or your heart beats
the answer to a hard question

when your shoulders tell you (again and again)
what you're holding is too heavy
or when your soul sings as you write
just the right words

I know you weren't taught how to listen
to her, weren't taught how she works
only taught to keep her covered
and skinny (but not too skinny)

but you're both older and wiser now
and she's talking and you're listening
and there has never been
a more holy union

Michelle Windsor

A Married Thursday, Nine Years In

You
never—
Why
can't
you—
Let's
try—
Same
team—
I
see
you—
Begin
again.

Amy Grass

**In A World Where You Can
Be Anything, Be Weak**

Feel frailty throbbing
through your fingers,
touch your translucent
skin, wink at the wrinkles
whispering around your smile.

Lie down your limp limbs,
cry into your cup of tea,
treat yourself gently,
like someone you love.

Say, *this is hard*, say,
I am tired, say, *thank you*
to a meal, warm cookies,
soft, folded hand-me-downs,
and someone else's strong hands
buckling babies into car seats.

Mercy can't seep into your skin
if there's no cracks in the armour.

Rebecca Fergie

Planning on Wrinkles

I plan to be an old woman.

I plan to wear silver wires
well past my shoulders,
while inviting a murder
to nest on either side of my eyes.

I plan to look the part of wisdom
and act like a child
any gosh darn time I feel like it,
because I can't imagine a wiser way
to stay lost and alive in the woods.

I plan to blow the dust off a new book
and try my elbows at tennis,
or the steady arms of a rocking chair
on a wraparound porch.

I plan to have hands
with silky deltas fingering out
to half hoist babes this way to heaven,
from this side of the soil.

I plan to have wrinkles so supple and so deep.
My brow will insist on waders and teenage birthday suits.
Because its waters will lap
the thighs of anglers and lovers,
both casting lines to catch

something

to release.

Megan Sciarrino

ABOUT THE AUTHORS

Part-Time Poets is a collaborative monthly Substack publication and is home to poetry born in the margins of to-do lists and note apps in pickup lines. It's where you'll find poems that started as a word traced on the shower wall or scribbled on a scrap of paper at 3:00 a.m. It's where words are inspired by the reality of crumbs on the floor and dreams of a better future. It's a home for stories of hope, grief and everything in between. You can find us at parttimepoets.substack.com.

Alyssa Silvester is a Type-A Midwesterner who cares for her people through home-cooked meals and words of affirmation. She lives in Hoover, Alabama—a born Michigander turned Washingtonian turned Southerner through her family's journey in military medicine—with her husband, children (son and daughter 20 months apart), and two cats. Alyssa loves a good spreadsheet, seasonal decorations and foods, great books, and her Peloton streak. You can connect with her on Substack alyssasilvester.substack.com and Instagram @aasilvester.

Amy Grass is a wife and mom of three in St. Louis, Missouri. When she's not writing poetry about the ordinary moments of motherhood, she can be found baking layer cakes, catching up with friends on a morning run, or working her way through her ever-growing stack of library books. You can connect with Amy on Substack amygrass.substack.com or on Instagram @amyegrass.

Rebecca Fergie lives in Perth, Western Australia with her husband and their three boys. She spends her days counselling, teaching women the Bible, coordinating an evangelistic playgroup, and writing. She is a regular contributor to Part Time Poets and The Gospel Coalition Australia. Her spiritual gift is losing things. You can find more at The Sunday Morning Snuggle on Substack thesundaymorningsnuggle.substack.com.

Jillian Stacia wants to live in a world where the coffee is bottomless and the sweatpants are mandatory. She spends her days crafting creative copy for clients in Children's Programming. Her poetry and creative nonfiction essays have been featured in Querencia Press, Plentitude Journal, Remington Review, Coffee & Crumbs, and Voicemail Poems. When she's not writing, Jillian can be found snuggling with her two adorable children and cheering on the Baltimore Ravens. You can find her on Instagram @jillianstacia.

Krista Drechsel is a writer, teacher, wife and mother in Minneapolis. If she's not spending time outside, you can find her drinking coffee, writing, or staying up way too late with a book. She believes in the power of words to help us feel seen, held, and loved. You can find more of her work on Substack substack.com/@kristadrechsel.

Lorren Lemmons is a freelance writer and mother of three. After years of moving around the United States as a military spouse, her family has settled down in her hometown in Idaho. She was the deputy editor of *WRKWNDR Magazine* during its four-year publication run, is a copy editor for Wayfare, and is on the poetry board of Segullah. In addition to Part-Time Poets, her poetry, essays, and short fiction have been published in Psaltery & Lyre, Dialogue, Wayfare, Exponent II, Literary Mama, Coffee + Crumbs, and other publications. She is working on her first novel. You can find her on Instagram and Threads @lorrenlemmons and on Substack at lorrenlemmons.substack.com.

Megan Sciarrino is a nonprofit writer who appeals to folks to care about the planet (and really hopes it works). She prefers to find her breath outside, with her camera in tow, ever hopeful to catch the places where the light lands. She married for laughs, lives to love her favorite people, and poetry might be her first language. You can find her on Instagram @maggybeegoing.

Michelle Windsor is a full-time thinker, part-time writer who writes poems because an essay doesn't fit on a shower wall. She is the creator of Part-Time Poets and shares her poems on Substack michellevwindsor.substack.com and Instagram @michellewindsor.

Taylor Epperson is a poet, romance author, and lover of words. She lives with her husband and daughter in northern Colorado, where she is attending college to become a high school English teacher. When she's not writing, she can often be found perusing the pages of a cookbook and trying out new recipes. You can connect with her on Substack tayepperson.substack.com or Instagram @authortaylorepperson.

Made in the USA
Coppell, TX
14 February 2025